Loveless

ITISH PANDE

Woven Words Publishers OPC Pvt. Ltd.

Registered Office:

Vill: Raipur, P.O: Raipur Paschimbar,

Dist: Purba Midnapore, Pin: 721401,

West Bengal, India.

Branch Office(Operations): Hyderabad

www.wovenwordspublishers.com

Email: publish@wovenwordspublishers.com

First published by Woven Words Publishers OPC Pvt. Ltd., 2019

Copyright© Itish Pande, 2019

POETRY

IMPRINT: WOVEN WORDS FIRE

ISBN 13: 978-93-86897-99-2

ISBN 10: 93-86897-99-7

Price: $ 6/ 200 INR

Printed and bound in India by Woven Words Publishers.

Introduction

This book contains writings about my infatuation that I had at the age of 14.

It will tell you about my "love" story in the form of poems and quotes, all in a particular order.

Hope you enjoy ;)

Acknowledgements

Oh! This is the part where I am supposed to show my gratitude to people who have helped me in making Loveless an actual book from an almost discarded idea it was earlier? So, let's be dead honest then, no formalities.

Thank you Mumma for being my encouragement throughout the whole process

Thank you, Papa, for helping me with everything.

And Thank you to my special fellas out there who supported me, right from when it all started. (You know who you are!!)

And a very very humble and loved thanks to the Woven Words team for publishing this.

I Love You people, and I wouldn't be here, without your support.

Part1:

The Beginning

Love at The First Glance

It was winter when I saw you
for the first time
I looked at you
and you looked at me
Oh boy! That look of yours straight
into my eyes, made me freeze
Just like the cold breeze

You smiled and so did I
At that time, I just wanted to come to you and
say "Hi"
But I did not, because I was an Idiot
and I was shy

As you sat in your car, you gave me
another smile, and I just thought of
two things, all day, all while
"Had I missed my chance?
Had I fallen for you, at the first glance?"

The Move

The next day I stood at the same place, hoping
for you to come, and you did!
I had to be a man, and not a kid
I had to talk to you that day, no matter what
And in my mind, that was the only thought

You saw me coming your way and you
smiled once again
It felt like your smile had cured all my pain
My brain literally froze
and my heart lost its beat
My steps I just couldn't retreat
But I kept walking towards you
Probably my heart knew
what it was making me do
Probably it had found its perfect match

I tried talking to you, but you simply laughed
at my nervousness
But one thing was for sure, I had fallen for
you, really hard and bad
It's almost a year today since I met you I am
happy, I feel lucky and I am glad!

Admiration

You came into my life, just like the other girls
Your eyes so beautiful, your hair full of curls

There was something special about you
You were different, unlike the rest
Stupid, Idiotic, Childish and Lame, but to me
you turned out to be the best

I remember looking at you for the first time
When everything around me had gone silent
It felt like the time had stopped.
The weather got cooler, maybe, the
temperature had dropped

As you went away, I kept thinking about you
all night and all day
I wanted you to be my friend
To be honest, I never wanted
that moment to end

Wish I could capture it
Wish I could play it over and over again
You seemed to be the cure to all my bane
I had probably fallen in love with you, and all
I remember is that after that day
I had gone insane

The Castles

How happy can I be for the fact
that we have become one
I'm sure, we will be different
and it will be too much fun
I would do anything to keep you happy
and will make sure to brighten your mood
whenever you get snappy

Your smile brightens up my day
I am going crazy behind you
is what my friends say
I'll never let anything negative
come in our way
And so I promise you that

Whenever you'll need me
I'll always be there
For you, I'll always care
And I'm sure, we'll be a perfect pair

The Absurd Attitude

I don't know why, but
you have started behaving strange
There's something wrong with your attitude
I can see that there's a change

You have stopped talking properly, and I
don't know why is that
I wait for you to come online at nights, but
you've stopped to chat

Neither do you tell me the problem
and nor do you talk
When you see me coming your way, you
turn around and just begin to walk

This has put me in a state of worry
I am unable to concentrate
and am always in a hurry

I wonder what the problem is and why you
are behaving this way
do you even love me?
or that's just something, you say?

Realisation

It was never you
It was always me, who was mad behind you
and was stuck like glue

I never realised what I was doing or why I
came to you at the first place
I know I am insane, because when you'll go
you're the one I'll trace
I'll always remember that face
Those eyes, lips and smile
That killed me every while
Making my heart melt
whenever I was angry or sad
Putting me into a good mood from a bad
I was just too attached to you
But now I just love you less
Because you have put me into a mess
I just never deserved you, probably
I didn't want you to be someone else's
Hence I tried to reserve you

It was a mistake that I made
Maybe the hormones
which gushed like crazy
I just wanted somcone to understand me

but you never did
It was my inner self that I hid
Who kept telling me to "Wake up"
Girl, your love had made me blind
And all I did this while, was whined

The Fake Consolation

Things have become fine
Once again, I can proudly say that
"Yes, you are mine"

We argued and we fought
We were hurt, and thus this relationship is
currently tied with a "knot"

You are the one and you'll always be
Because with your love and support
I become a better me

Every couple fights and so did we
It did not turn out to be as worst as
I thought it would be

So, now my soul has mate
And we will never leave each other and
let me get that straight

The Dilemma

I am currently in that stage of my life
Where, I don't know what I am doing
Where I am completely clueless
Where I can see myself change

This is maybe just the teenage
That has filled me up with rage
I control my anger inside me, as if it were an
animal inside a cage

I am in a situation, I am in a mess
I don't know what it is
Hence, I'm trying to make a guess

I gotta work, I gotta do more
Because I know that the opportunity won't
always be there, knocking at my door

The Sad Reality

As I started crying
My feelings started dying
I said I was happy, I said I was fine
Though somewhere inside me
I knew I was lying
I didn't want to end it, I didn't want to hurt
you, so I kept on trying

But for how long could it last?
One day eventually, I had to blast
And so I did
I told you everything that I had in me
These troublesome feelings I hid

Instead of being sad
You seemed to not care at all
Not even by a tad
I was completely wrong
And I realized that
your love made me weak, not strong

It definitely didn't turn out the way how I
imagined it to be
But one thing's for sure
Without you, I did become a better me

The Whining

I was an immature fool
Who wanted a girlfriend
probably just to look cool

I did get you, but
you completely changed my life

I had got so infatuated that for once
I thought that you would be my future wife.
You came into my life with your problems
and I made them as mine
I never slept unless I made sure
that you were fine

At the end of everything,
my love for you was said to be "bad".
I wouldn't hesitate to agree with that because
it had made me completely mad

You went away from my life, and left me
alone in all this mess
All of your "deeds" that I have told the readers
through this poem, are yet very, very less

All the things that I did for you
were worthless
From the writing pages, to those cheesy text
messages, being "nice", "supportive"
"helpful" and "caring"...
Ahh, thinking of that now
makes me cringe and feel so cheap
But I probably always will for some time
because the wounds that you have given me
are deep

Your ignorance and words
cut me deeper than a knife
But they also made me strong
And at the end of that day, you "Won" and I
was proved to be "Wrong"

Being with you is of what, I kept dreaming
Little did I know, all this time, all this while
Because of you, my heart just kept screaming

The "Break Up"

Part 2:

The Aftermath

Obnoxious Nights

I don't know what happens to me every night
I feel weird, I feel emotional
I just don't feel right

I lie on the bed staring at the ceiling
Wondering what's wrong
why I get that feeling

I know it's temporary and it will fade away
I try to sleep, but my brain doesn't let me
and reminds me of you which makes me
regret that I should have asked you to stay

That disturbs me inside somewhere
I get breathless and
I start looking here and there

I may try to act apathetic, but due to these
feelings, I always fail
And at the end of the day, it turns out to be
yet another "fairy tale"

The Hatred

It burns my heart when I think about you
I shouldn't be doing that, but sometimes
that is what I do

It took time for me to understand what you
were doing to me
"Us" didn't turn out the way
how I imagined it to be

You just got pain into my life and nothing
more than that
Wish I had listened to my inner self, who just
wanted you to scat

Your attitude and behaviour made me go mad
Somehow, I managed to get rid of you, it was
tough it was painful
But now I am at peace, and I am glad

The Memories

Why is it that you are still in my head?
Why is it that I still think of you
when I lie on the bed?
Why is it that you still exist for me, even
though I said that, for me, you were dead?

Why is it that I am unable to move on?
Why is it that I still
think of us as one, and mourn?
Why is it that I sometimes feel your presence
around me, even though you have gone

Why is it that I am failing
to use my own advice
I am in search for answers, but as of now, If I
don't stop, I'll probably end up
causing my own demise

Unnecessary Guilt

There's nothing I can do
About the words I said

There's nothing I can do
About my feelings which are dead

There's nothing I can do
About the involuntary feelings that come out
when I lie on the bed

There's nothing I can do
About the hate between us, which spread

But if there's something I can do
Is to forget about you, and
rather focus on what's ahead

Despair

And now these emotions are
getting too much to bear
I am suppressed by them, unable to do
anything, feeling bizarre

They make me go through my past
Which ends up making me
think about it eventually
And I wonder why it still hurts
even though I said I didn't care

I need to find a solution
I need to help myself
I need to learn how to control these feelings
Because if I don't
I'll probably end up in despair

Letting Go

Hopeless, I tried going back to sleep
I promised myself that about you
I would no longer weep

Scared, I closed my eyes
Trying my best, to not think about you
and neither about your lies

Breathless, I got up again
and leaned against the window pane
Thinking about all this
and what exactly did I gain?

Exhausted, I tried to sleep one more time
and went back to bed
Encouraged myself to let go of you
and to get you out of my head

Slowly, I fell asleep
To not cry about you, was a promise I made
to myself that I was determined to keep
In order to once again, grow and to reap

Haunting

The next morning, I woke up, feeling a little
different, a little relieved
I had moved on, is what I told myself and is
what I wish everyone believed

They would take your name, just to see how
much it affected me
And I bravely, used to continue talking,
showing that it didn't
and that I was finally free

But yet once again, I only was fooling myself
even when I didn't intend to
Maybe somewhere, it still hurt me
And probably, it was true

Downhearted, I didn't know what to do
Wondering, about how longer would
this haunting continue

I would eventually one day get over you
I had to try, to start a life, to build a me
a one which was better
and a one which was new

Part 3:

Reminiscence

I Came to you-
Wretched and in need of love. But you ended
up making the condition worse
by traumatizing me and
making me loose faith in love

I never knew what pain
and agony felt like
Until I met you
I never knew how being in despair
and getting lost felt like
Until I met you
I never knew what depression
and torture felt like
Until I met You
Neither did I know that
I had a poet hiding inside me
Until I met you

They say life knocks us down
really bad sometimes
You knocked me down too
really hard and bad

–My "life"

Your Love had blinded me enough, to engulf
me in a world where there was only misery
dilemmas and confusion

We were two people intertwined as one
living a happy life, in a reality
which did not exist

I always used to run away from my problems
but unfortunately, I failed
to run away from you

I thought you added light to my life, but in reality, you ended up taking it all away

The more I indulged
myself in you, the further
I drifted apart from reality
walking away from
everything and everything that I had

You slithered up to my heart, wrapped
yourself around it and burst it open
just like a snake

–Anaconda

Your love might have failed in bringing out
the best in me, but your harsh words and
asperous attitude succeeded in doing so

*- I looked for the positive
in the negative things you did.*

*Probably, the one major difference between
us*

It's funny how you crushed my heart but it
still couldn't stop dancing because of you

And as I lay there hopelessly, helplessly
My mind traumatised.
My heart breaking
What got me back to reality
was hope and love-
given by the people around me
and it healed the wounds
caused by you

-Love Hurts, Love Heals

You went-
Away from my life, as if you had never come
Away from my heart, making it numb
taking not the whole of it though, but some

I let myself drown in your anguish and yet
today I wonder why I did that

-*"Maybe I wanted a girlfriend, just to look
cool"*

In my darkest times
when I needed you
You weren't there

In my happiest times
When I needed you
You weren't there
In my most helpless times
when I needed you
You weren't there

-The fact is; You were never there
Whenever I needed you
Whenever you were supposed to be

The day when I first saw you
and the day when I last
talked to you, were both
indeed beautiful days

Every time I thought about you
There used to come a feeling somewhere from
the bottom of my heart
telling me to regain practicality
But I was so overwhelmed by these emotions
that i refused to listen to myself

Every time I saw you
There used to come a feeling telling me that
you weren't the right choice, but i was so
crazy behind that smile of yours
that I used to shut myself up

Every time I talked about you
My friends, always gave a hopeless reaction
constantly telling me how blinded I was
But I always, always shrugged them off, fake
consoling myself, leading myself into deeper
and deeper depths of despair

How much did you lie, when you
said that you loved me?
How much did you lie, when you
said that you needed me?
How much did you lie, when you
said that you cared for me?
How much did you lie, when you
said that I was the one
your soul loved?
How much did you lie, when you
said that we would last forever?

I was so wrong when
I trusted you blindly, thinking you would
never betray or hurt me
I was so wrong when
I chose you over everybody else, thinking you
would stay with me forever
I was so wrong when
I used to feel happy
thinking you were the perfect one
And I was so wrong when I was ready to give
you my everything, thinking you deserved it

I knew it was time–
When I could see myself drowning in misery

I knew it was time–
When I could see myself changing, and
becoming a different person
drifting into an unreal fantasy

I knew it was time–
When I no longer felt happy around you

I knew it was time–
When all that I saw was darkness and
hopelessness whenever I envisioned us
together in future

I knew it was time
For me, to finally, get rid, of you

I should have realized it earlier by what you
meant when you said that you loved me
I should have realized it earlier
what you were doing to me
and what was going on
I should have realized it earlier
what you were turning me into, because of
the tribulation you had become
I should have realized that all you
did was put me in vexation

I should have realized
I should have

What did you mean when you said
that you loved me?

Were you telling me something
that you didn't do?

Were you giving me false hopes, enough to
let me make air castles and
dance in my own fantasies?

Or did you actually mean it?

From your actions, I could read that you were
just lying, straight from the beginning

What was wrong with me when I failed to
listen to myself
and rather chose to fall for you?

What was wrong with me when I went
against my friends and
rather chose to stand with you?

What was wrong with me, when I kept
making a fool out of myself saying
that you loved me?

You know what was wrong? −You

My soul must have smiled
the day I accepted the
bitter truth, by
letting go of my
ego and
stubbornness

-Letting Go

While I was with you
I used to wonder if your love
for me ever existed
And after you left
I used to wonder if love
Really ever existed

-Perspectives Change

I had fantasized us to such an
extent that now, when I try to
think of anything related to it, my mind
brings up your face in front of my eyes
your laughing and happy voice
plays in my ears
and it gives me a synopsis of
everything I thought about
with you and it makes me
wonder-

Did I really love you or it
was just the infatuation?

And at the end of the
day, I get confused
sometimes wondering
if it was your fault or mine?
Was it me who had
gone mad behind you, by completely
ignoring the reality?
or was it you who did that to me
knowing what I was doing
for you?

-You could have been nice or
Maybe I should have realized
Everything quicker

And even after you have gone away from my
life, you still continue to
lead me into dilemmas

Your heart could never
understand what was going
on in my head and my
brain could never
understand what was going on in your heart.

*"Does she even love me? Does she
even understand my problems"
— A question I often asked
myself*

*"Yes she does"— Me feeding
myself lies just like every other night*

Thinking back to the old
days, I don't really find your "doing"
to be something
really disastrous.
What you did, and the way you behaved was
definitely not how a "girlfriend" or
even a "best friend" would
behave, but for a fourteen
year old kid, especially for
an over emotional one
it was a lot.

It's funny how I cried with the fear of losing
you, thinking my life revolved around you
and losing you would be
as good as losing my world

But it's pathetic and stupid that I failed to
realize that I had already lost my world when I
chose you over them

Getting emotional sometimes
when I try to reminisce about
us, I don't see anything.
Because how could I indulge myself in sweet
memories of us or recollect about our
enjoyable moments when there weren't any
at the first place?

I didn't realize or maybe
I didn't
accept anything
you were doing
because I was scared that I
would end up losing you and
I wondered how I would
handle myself after that.

-Silly Fear of a 14-year-old

I've come to that stage
now that even if I try to
write about you, there's
nothing that comes out
from me.
There's no more hatred
There are more grudges.
What's left are some "sweet childish"
memories and gratefulness.

How ironic of us it was
You took in the hate in all the love
I threw towards
you and I tried to find the
love in all the hate you
threw towards me

As you faded away
from my arms
I realized what I had
been holding onto
wasn't you, but was a
reflection of what we
could have been

How ironic of us again
I gave you the
attention you never
deserved and you gave me
the attention that I didn't deserve

I could-
Have stopped you- From leaving
Have stopped me- From bearing
Have stopped us- From growing

But- I let it happen
Maybe because I knew it was time
For you- To finally go
And For me-
To finally grow

Your eyes and smile
could make a fool out of a
14 year old kid
making his heart melt.
But they could not do the
same to a 16-year-old

It's surprising how I still manage to
write about you sometimes.
I think there's nothing that's left.
But every time I
close my eyes, there's always
something my memories show me
There's always
something those
over exaggerated wounds remind
me, and there's always something
which just doesn't stop me, from
writing about you
even though it's not needed.

I may have cursed love a lot, but
Actually, it was me just cursing
    you in different ways

- *How else would a 14 year old satisfy
  his ego?*

How silly and stupid of me it was
to curse you so much
forgetting about the fact
that you too were a 13
year old trying to figure
out and fight with more
complicated things in life

I had thought a lot about us.
I wished for us to be beautiful
iconic and admiring.
But it's okay that it couldn't
turn out that way, because
sometimes life doesn't go
the way you want it to.
And probably there's nothing
that you can do about it, rather than
to learn to accept it, and move on.

*-After all we both were kids, immature and
fighting with our own demons*

Even though we couldn't be
the ideal "partners"
we were beautiful
in our own fantasies.
From the excitement in our
eyes when we looked at
each other, to the
impatience of growing up
and being together.
From those future plans to
those late-night talks
which though was Impractical
but can be called cute.

Even though there
were hardly any good days
I did enjoy that
feeling of "love" and
getting to call
someone as my "own"
Ignoring the fact that
it though turned out
to be disastrous, it was
beautiful in its own
limited time period.

And I can finally say that now
I have come to that point where
I can no longer write about
you and no longer feel the need to.
Mistakes have been accepted
Misunderstandings have been
cleared
The past has been
forgotten and there's nothing
that's left which would make
me further want to curse you.

-What's left are some
"sweet childish memories and gratefulness"